MISSAL

✠

The Order of Mass in English

THIS BOOK SUPPLIES THE ORDER OF MASS (*Ordo Missæ*) of the Latin Rite exactly as it is given in the Roman Missal (*Missale Romanum*) of 1969 with the variations specified in the second edition of 1975. It follows the translation approved by the National Conference of Catholic Bishops and confirmed by the Holy See.

In this edition, the pattern of sense lines, capitalization, and other matters of style follow the conventions mandated by the International Commission on English in the Liturgy. Some of the rubrics that do not direct the actions or gestures of the people have been omitted or condensed; others have been expanded by the addition of certain passages from the *General Instruction of the Roman Missal* that are incorporated by reference in that approved translation. Certain explanatory passages from the *General Instruction*, here printed in black type, have been interposed as seems helpful; the *General Instruction* itself should be consulted. The guidelines for receiving the Blessed Sacrament, promulgated by The National Conference of Catholic Bishops, Washington, D.C., in November, 1996, have also been inserted.

Passages that vary according to the season have been distinguished here by horizontal brackets. A cross (✠) in the text indicates the gesture of blessing by the priest. Places in the text at which proper names are to be inserted are indicated by the symbol N.

The Proper of the Mass, which includes the readings from the Bible and certain prayers that change each day of the year and according to the season, feast, ritual, or occasion celebrated, may be found in approved Lectionaries and Missals. The locations of the elements of the Proper within the Order of Mass are designated here by the notation Of the Proper.

Canon 838 directs that "it is for the Holy See to order the sacred liturgy of the Universal Church, to publish the liturgical books, to review their translations into the vernacular language, and to see that liturgical ordinances are faithfully observed everywhere."

The Apostolic Constitution *Sacrosanctum Concilium* (22:3) specifies that "no other person, not even if he is a priest, may on his own add, remove, or change anything in the liturgy."

However, certain elements of the Order of Mass vary according to the season and the intention of the Mass, and the priest may select one of several optional prayers at certain designated parts of the Mass, according with Canon Law and the norms given in the *General Instruction*. These options are indicated here by Roman numerals or capital letters.

The *General Instruction* also assigns to the priest responsibility for pronouncing, at his option, the instructions and words of introduction and conclusion that are provided in the rites themselves; these need not be expressed verbatim as they are given in the Roman

Missal, and the priest may adapt them to the concrete situation of the community. The *Instruction* also allows that the priest may give the people a brief introduction to the Mass of the day before the celebration begins, to the Liturgy of the Word before the readings, and to the Eucharistic Prayer before the Preface.

Sacrosanctum Concilium advises that short directives of a more explicitly liturgical nature may be spoken by the priest or a competent minister, but only at suitable moments and only in the prescribed words or their equivalent. Those elements of the Mass itself that may be expressed in this way by the priest are indicated in the rubrics by the notation "these or similar words".

The Instruction of Pope Paul VI, 5 September 1970, on the orderly carrying out of the provisions of *Sacrosanctum Concilium* admonished that to go beyond the defined limits "would be to strip the liturgy of its sacred symbolism and proper beauty … accordingly the rites must retain their dignity, spirit of reverence, and sacred character. … Keep in mind, then, that the private recasting of ritual introduced by an individual priest insults the dignity of the believer".

Concordat cum originali:
Reverend James P. Moroney
Executive Director
Secretariat for the Liturgy
National Conference of Catholic Bishops

Liturgical texts are released
by the National Conference of Catholic Bishops,
confirmed by the Apostolic See, and published
by authority of the Bishops' Committee on the Liturgy.

Published in the United States of America
May 13, 1997
by
Pangæus Press
Post Office Box 670127
Dallas, Texas 75367-0127 U.S.A.

ISBN 0-9653660-2-2

Library of Congress Card Catalog Number 96-72357

Design by David Lloyd Beck, Dallas

Manufactured in the United States of America

THE ORDER OF MASS

INTRODUCTORY RITES

After the people have assembled for Mass, an entrance song begins as the priest and ministers enter. This song is to open the celebration of the Mass, intensify the unity of the assembled people, lead their thoughts to the mystery of the season or feast, and accompany the procession of priest and ministers.

Entrance Song

After the entrance song, everyone makes the sign of the cross.

Priest: In the name of the Father, and of the Son, and of the Holy Spirit.

People: Amen.

Greeting

Then the priest, facing the people, extends his hands and greets all present with one of the following greetings.

A Priest: The grace of our Lord Jesus Christ and the love of God and the fellowship of the Holy Spirit be with you all.

People: And also with you.

B Priest: The grace and peace of God our Father and the Lord Jesus Christ be with you.

People: Blessed be God, the Father of our Lord Jesus Christ.

or: And also with you.

C Priest: The Lord be with you. (A bishop says Peace be with you.)

People: And also with you.

The priest, deacon, or other suitable minister may very briefly introduce the Mass of the day. Either the rite of blessing and sprinkling or the penitential rite follows.

A RITE OF BLESSING AND SPRINKLING HOLY WATER

When this rite is celebrated it takes the place of the penitential rite at the beginning of Mass. The Kyrie is also omitted.

After greeting the people, the priest remains standing at his chair. A vessel containing the water to be blessed is placed before him. Facing the people, he invites them to pray, using these or similar words:

Priest: Dear friends,
this water will be used
to remind us of our baptism.
Let us ask God to bless it,
and to keep us faithful
to the Spirit he has given us.

After a brief silence, he joins his hands and continues, using one of the following prayers:

A God our Father,
your gift of water
brings life and freshness to the earth;

it washes away our sins
and brings us eternal life.

We ask you now
to bless ✠ this water,
and to give us your protection on this day
which you have made your own.
Renew the living spring of your life within us
and protect us in spirit and body,
that we may be free from sin
and come into your presence
to receive the gift of salvation.

We ask this through Christ our Lord.

B Lord God almighty,
creator of all life,
of body and soul,
we ask you to bless ✠ this water
as we use it in faith:
forgive our sins
and save us from all illness
and the power of evil.

Lord,
in your mercy
give us living water,
always springing up as a fountain of salvation:
free us, body and soul, from every danger,
and admit us to your presence
in purity of heart.

Grant this through Christ our Lord.

C (during the Easter season)

Lord God almighty,
hear the prayers of your people:
we celebrate our creation and redemption.
Hear our prayers and bless ✠ this water,
which gives fruitfulness to the fields,
and refreshment and cleansing to man.
You chose water to show your goodness
when you led your people to freedom
through the Red Sea
and satisfied their thirst in the desert
with water from the rock.
Water was the symbol used by the prophets
to foretell your new covenant with man.
You made the water of baptism holy
by Christ's baptism in the Jordan:
by it you give us a new birth
and renew us in holiness.
May this water remind us of our baptism,
and let us share the joy
of all who have been baptized at Easter.

We ask this through Christ our Lord.

Taking the sprinkler, the priest sprinkles himself and his ministers, the rest of the clergy, and the people, while an appropriate song or antiphon is sung.

When he returns to his place and the song is finished, the priest faces the people and, with joined hands, says:

May almighty God cleanse us of our sins,
and through the eucharist we celebrate
make us worthy to sit at his table

in his heavenly kingdom.

The people respond:

Amen.

When it is prescribed, the Gloria is then sung or said.

B PENITENTIAL RITE

The priest may use any of these three forms or similar words.

A As we prepare to celebrate this mystery of Christ's love,
let us acknowledge our failures
and ask God for pardon and strength.

B Coming together as God's family,
with confidence let us ask the Father's forgiveness,
for he is full of gentleness and compassion.

C My brothers and sisters

(or, at his discretion, friends, dearly beloved, brethren, or other words more suitable to the occasion)

to prepare ourselves to celebrate the sacred mysteries,
let us call to mind our sins.

A pause for silent reflection follows.

After the silence, one of the following three penitential prayers is chosen.

A All say:

I confess to almighty God,
and to you, my brothers and sisters,
that I have sinned through my own fault

They strike themselves on the breast:

in my thoughts and in my words,

in what I have done,
and in what I have failed to do;
and I ask blessed Mary, ever virgin,
all the angels and saints,
and you, my brothers and sisters,
to pray for me to the Lord our God.

B Priest: Lord, we have sinned against you:
Lord, have mercy.

People: Lord, have mercy.

Priest: Lord, show us your mercy and love.

People: And grant us your salvation.

C The priest or other suitable minister may make the following or similar invocations, eight of which are found in the Roman Missal.

Priest: You were sent to heal the contrite:
Lord, have mercy.

People: Lord, have mercy.

Priest: You came to call sinners:
Christ, have mercy.

People: Christ, have mercy.

Priest: You plead for us at the right hand of the Father:
Lord, have mercy.

People: Lord, have mercy.

After any of these forms:

Priest: May almighty God have mercy on us,
forgive us our sins,
and bring us to everlasting life.

People: Amen.

Unless the third form of penitential prayer is used, the Kyrie or Lord, Have Mercy is sung or said by all, in English or in Greek, with the choir or cantor alternating with the people:

Priest or other minister: Lord, have mercy.

People: Lord, have mercy.

Priest or other minister: Christ, have mercy.

People: Christ, have mercy.

Priest or other minister: Lord, have mercy.

People: Lord, have mercy.

Or:

Priest: Kyrie, eleison.

People: Kyrie, eleison.

Priest: Christe, eleison.

People: Christe, eleison.

Priest: Kyrie, eleison.

People: Kyrie, eleison.

GLORIA

The Gloria is sung or said on Sundays outside Advent and Lent, on solemnities and feasts, and in special, more solemn celebrations. The priest or cantor may begin it, or all may begin it together; it is sung by the people alone or alternately with the choir, or by the choir alone. If it is not sung, it is said by all together or in alternation.

Glory to God in the highest,
and peace to his people on earth.

Lord God, heavenly King,
almighty God and Father,
  we worship you, we give you thanks,
  we praise you for your glory.

Lord Jesus Christ, only Son of the Father,
Lord God, Lamb of God,
you take away the sin of the world:
  have mercy on us;
you are seated at the right hand of the Father:
  receive our prayer.

For you alone are the Holy One,
you alone are the Lord,
you alone are the Most High,
  Jesus Christ,
  with the Holy Spirit,
  in the glory of God the Father. Amen.

Opening Prayer

The priest, with hands joined, sings or says:

Priest: Let us pray.

Priest and people pray silently for a moment. Then the priest says the opening prayer ("collect") proper to the Mass and concludes it:

Priest: … for ever and ever.

People: Amen.

THE LITURGY OF THE WORD

The Liturgy of the Word includes readings from the Bible, selected thematically as appropriate to the Mass and usually consisting of a reading from the Old Testament, a psalm in which the people respond to the verses, a reading from one of the apostles, and a reading from a gospel.

When the Scriptures are read in the Church, God himself is speaking to his people, and Christ, present in his own word, is proclaiming the gospel. In the Biblical readings God's word addresses all people of every era and is understandable to them.

The readings must, therefore, be listened to by all with proper reverence.

First Reading

Of the Proper. At the end of the reading:

Reader: The Word of the Lord.

People: Thanks be to God.

Responsorial Psalm

Of the Proper.

The psalmist or cantor sings the verses of the psalm at the lectern or at another suitable place. If the psalm is sung through without the response, the people remain seated and listen. Often, the cantor sings the verse of response once and the people repeat it, and then all respond with that verse to each verse that the cantor sings, as directed.

SECOND READING

When there is a second reading, it is of the Proper. At the end of the reading:

Reader: The Word of the Lord.

People: Thanks be to God.

ALLELUIA OR GOSPEL ACCLAMATION

The alleluia or other chant follows. It is to be omitted if it is not sung.

If a deacon is to proclaim the gospel, he comes before the priest, bows, and asks his blessing:

Deacon: Father, give me your blessing.

The priest responds in a low voice:

Priest: The Lord be in your heart and on your lips that you may worthily proclaim his gospel. In the name of the Father, and of the Son, ✠ and of the Holy Spirit.

Deacon: Amen.

If there is no deacon, the priest bows before the altar and says inaudibly:

Priest: Almighty God, cleanse my heart and my lips that I may worthily proclaim your gospel.

Then the deacon (or the priest) goes to the lectern. He may be accompanied by ministers with incense and candles.

GOSPEL

The liturgy itself communicates the great reverence to be shown to the reading of the gospel, setting it off from the other readings with special marks of honor.

Priest or deacon: The Lord be with you.

People: And also with you.

Priest or deacon: A reading from the holy gospel according to N.

People: Glory to you, O Lord.

If incense is used, the deacon or priest incenses the book and proclaims the gospel, which is of the Proper.

At the end of the gospel reading:

Priest or deacon: The gospel of the Lord.

People: Praise to you, Lord Jesus Christ.

The priest or deacon kisses the book of the gospel, saying inaudibly:

May the words of the gospel wipe away our sins.

Homily

The homily is an integral part of the liturgy. It is given on Sundays and holy days of obligation at all Masses that are celebrated with a congregation; it may not be omitted without a serious reason.

A living commentary on the word, the homily increases the word's effectiveness. It should develop some point of the readings or of another text from the Order or the Proper of the Mass of the day, and it should take into account the mystery being celebrated and the needs proper to the listeners.

Profession of Faith

The profession of faith is said on Sundays and solemnities, and it may also be said in solemn local celebrations.

If it is sung, all may sing it together or in alternation. The Nicene Creed is usually used, but the Apostles' Creed may be said after the Homily in Masses with Children.

The Nicene Creed

We believe in one God,
the Father, the Almighty,
maker of heaven and earth,
of all that is seen and unseen.

We believe in one Lord, Jesus Christ,
  the only Son of God,
  eternally begotten of the Father,
  God from God, Light from Light,
  true God from true God,
  begotten, not made, one in Being with the Father.
  Through him all things were made.
  For us men and for our salvation
    he came down from heaven:

All bow during the next two lines.

by the power of the Holy Spirit
  he was born of the Virgin Mary, and became man.

For our sake he was crucified under Pontius Pilate;
  he suffered, died, and was buried.
  On the third day, he arose again
    in fulfillment of the Scriptures;
  he ascended into heaven
    and is seated at the right hand of the Father.
He will come again in glory to judge the living and
  the dead,
  and his kingdom will have no end.

We believe in the Holy Spirit, the Lord, the giver of life,
who proceeds from the Father and the Son.
With the Father and the Son he is worshipped and glorified.
He has spoken through the prophets.
We believe in one holy catholic and apostolic Church.
We acknowledge one baptism for the forgiveness of sins.
We look for the resurrection of the dead,
and the life of the world to come. Amen.

In celebrations of Masses with Children, the Apostles' Creed may be said after the homily.

I believe in God, the Father almighty,
creator of heaven and earth.

I believe in Jesus Christ, his only Son, our Lord.
He was conceived by the power of the Holy Spirit and born of the Virgin Mary.
He suffered under Pontius Pilate,
was crucified, died, and was buried.
He descended to the dead.
On the third day he rose again.
He ascended into heaven
and is seated at the right hand of the Father.
He will come again to judge the living and the dead.

I believe in the Holy Spirit,
the holy catholic Church,
the communion of saints,
the forgiveness of sins,
the resurrection of the body,
and the life everlasting. Amen.

General Intercessions

The priest presides at the prayer, giving a brief introduction and inviting the people to pray. It is desirable that the intentions be announced by a deacon, cantor, or other suitable person. The people express their supplication for these intentions either by a response said together after each intention or by silent prayer.

After the intentions, the priest says a concluding prayer.

LITURGY OF THE EUCHARIST

At the Last Supper, Christ instituted the sacrifice and paschal meal that makes the sacrifice of the Cross to be continuously present in the Church when the priest, representing Christ the Lord, carries out what the Lord did and handed over to his disciples to do in his memory.

Preparation of the Gifts

While the gifts of the people are brought forward to the priest and are placed on the altar, the offertory song is sung. It is desirable that the participation of the Faithful be expressed by members of the congregation bringing forward the bread and wine for the eucharist and the other gifts for the needs of the Church and the poor.

The priest, standing at the altar, takes the paten with the bread and, holding it slightly raised above the altar, says inaudibly:

> Blessed are you, Lord, God of all creation.
> Through your goodness we have this bread to offer,
> which earth has given and human hands have made.
> It will become for us the bread of life.

Then he places the paten with the bread on the corporal.

If there is no singing, the priest may say this prayer aloud, and the people may respond:

> Blessed be God for ever.

The deacon (or the priest) pours wine and a little water into the chalice, saying inaudibly:

> By the mystery of this water and wine may we come to share in the divinity of Christ, who humbled

himself to share in our humanity.

The priest takes the chalice and, holding it slightly raised above the altar, says inaudibly:

Blessed are you, Lord, God of all creation.
Through your goodness we have this wine to offer,
fruit of the vine and work of human hands.
It will become our spiritual drink.

Then he places the chalice on the corporal.

If there is no singing, the priest may say this prayer aloud, and the people may respond:

Blessed be God for ever.

The priest bows and says inaudibly:

Lord God, we ask you to receive us and be pleased with the sacrifice we offer you with humble and contrite hearts.

If incense is used, the priest may now incense the offerings and the altar, after which the deacon or a minister may incense the priest and the people.

The priest stands at the side of the altar and washes his hands, saying inaudibly:

Lord, wash away my iniquity; cleanse me from my sin.

Standing at the center of the altar, the priest faces the people. He extends and then joins his hands, saying:

Pray, brethren

(or friends*,* dearly beloved*, or* my brothers and sisters*)*,

that our sacrifice
may be acceptable to God, the almighty Father.

The people respond:

May the Lord accept the sacrifice at your hands
for the praise and glory of his name,
for our good, and the good of all his Church.

Prayer over the Gifts

The priest extends his hands and says the prayer over the gifts, concluding it:

… for ever and ever.

And the people respond:

Amen.

THE EUCHARISTIC PRAYER

The Roman Ritual specifies that the Lord and Savior Jesus Christ, present in the Sacrament, must be given the same worship and adoration that is to be given to God.

Priest: The Lord be with you.

People: And also with you.

Priest: Lift up your hearts.

People: We lift them up to the Lord.

Priest: Let us give thanks to the Lord our God.

People: It is right to give him thanks and praise.

PREFACE

The priest begins the preface, the first part of the eucharistic prayer, which varies according to the season, feast, or occasion that is celebrated and which eucharistic prayer is used. Eucharistic Prayer III may be used with any of the prefaces.

A (varies according to circumstances)

Father, all-powerful and ever-living God,
we do well always and everywhere to give you thanks …

B (usually with Eucharistic Prayer II)

Father, it is our duty and our salvation
always and everywhere
to give you thanks
through your beloved Son, Jesus Christ.

He is the Word through whom you made the universe,
the Savior you sent to redeem us.

By the power of the Holy Spirit,
he took flesh and was born of the Virgin Mary.

For our sake he opened his arms on the cross;
he put an end to death
and revealed the resurrection.
In this he fulfilled your will
and won for you a holy people.

And so we join the angels and the saints
in proclaiming your glory
as we say:

C (always with Eucharistic Prayer IV)

Father in heaven,
it is right that we should give you thanks and glory:
you are the one God, living and true.
Through all eternity you live in unapproachable light.
Source of all goodness, you have created all things,
to fill your creatures with every blessing
and lead all men to the joyful vision of your light.
Countless hosts of angels stand before you to do your will;
they look upon your splendor
and praise you, night and day.
United with them,
and in the name of every creature under heaven,
we too praise your glory as we say:

The priest concludes the preface by joining his hands and sings or says the Sanctus with the people.

SANCTUS

Holy, holy, holy Lord, God of power and might,
heaven and earth are full of your glory.

Hosanna in the highest.
Blessed is he who comes in the name of the Lord.
Hosanna in the highest.

The eucharistic prayer continues after the *Sanctus*.

I "We come to you, Father", page 21.

II "Lord, you are holy indeed", page 29.

III "Father, you are holy indeed", page 33.

IV "Father, we acknowledge", page 38.

The eucharistic prayers for Masses with Children, for Masses of Reconciliation, and for Masses for Various Needs and Occasions are also found in the Roman Missal.

I Eucharistic Prayer (The Roman Canon)

The words in brackets may be omitted.

The priest, with hands extended, says:

We come to you, Father,
with praise and thanksgiving,
through Jesus Christ, your Son.

He joins his hands and, making the sign of the cross once over both bread and chalice, says:

Through him we ask you to accept and bless ✠ these gifts we offer you in sacrifice.

With hands extended, he continues:

We offer them for your holy catholic Church;
watch over it, Lord, and guide it;
grant it peace and unity throughout the world.
We offer them for N. our Pope,
for N. our bishop

(or for N. our bishop and his assistant bishops)

and for all who hold and teach the catholic faith
that comes to us from the apostles.

Remember, Lord, your people,
especially those for whom we now pray, N. and N.

He prays for them briefly with his hands joined. Then, with hands extended, he continues:

Remember all of us gathered here before you.
You know how firmly we believe in you
and dedicate ourselves to you.
We offer this sacrifice of praise
for ourselves and those who are dear to us.

We pray to you, our living and true God,
for our well-being and redemption.

In union with the whole Church

From the Easter Vigil through the second Sunday of Easter:

we celebrate that day (or night)
when Jesus Christ, our Lord,
rose from the dead in his human body.

On the Feast of the Ascension:

we celebrate that day
when your Son, our Lord,
took his place with you
and raised our frail human nature to glory.

On Pentecost:

we celebrate the day of Pentecost
when the Holy Spirit appeared to the apostles
in the form of countless tongues.

we honor Mary,
the ever-virgin mother of Jesus Christ our Lord and God.

We honor Joseph, her husband,
the apostles and martyrs
Peter and Paul, Andrew,

[James, John, Thomas,
James, Philip,
Bartholomew, Matthew, Simon and Jude;
we honor Linus, Cletus, Clement, Sixtus,
Cornelius, Cyprian, Lawrence, Chrysogonus,
John and Paul, Cosmas and Damian,]

and all the saints.

May their merits and prayers
gain us your constant help and protection.

[Through Christ our Lord. Amen.]

With hands extended, he continues:

Father, accept this offering
from your whole family.

On Holy Thursday

in memory of the day when Jesus Christ, our Lord,
gave the mysteries of his body and blood
for his disciples to celebrate.

From the Easter Vigil through the second Sunday of Easter

and from those born into the new life
of water and the Holy Spirit,
with all their sins forgiven.

Grant us peace in this life,
save us from final damnation,
and count us among those you have chosen.

He joins his hands.

[Through Christ our Lord. Amen.]

With hands outstretched over the offerings, he says:

Bless and approve our offering;
make it acceptable to you,
an offering in spirit and in truth.
Let it become for us
the body and blood of Jesus Christ,

your only Son, our Lord.

He joins his hands.

[Through Christ our Lord. Amen.]

The words of the Lord in the following formulas should be spoken clearly and distinctly, as their meaning demands.

The day before he suffered

On Holy Thursday

to save us and all men,
that is today,

He takes the bread and, raising it a little above the altar, continues:

he took bread in his sacred hands

He looks upward.

and looking up to heaven,
to you, his almighty Father,
he gave you thanks and praise.
He broke the bread,
gave it to his disciples, and said,

He bows slightly.

Take this, all of you, and eat it:
this is my body which will be given up for you.

He shows the consecrated host to the people, places it on the paten, and genuflects in adoration. Then he continues:

When supper was ended,

He takes the chalice and, raising it a little above the altar, continues:

he took the cup.
Again he gave you thanks and praise,
gave the cup to his disciples, and said:

He bows slightly.

Take this, all of you, and drink from it:
this is the cup of my blood,
the blood of the new and everlasting covenant.
It will be shed for you and for all
so that sins may be forgiven.
Do this in memory of me.

He shows the chalice to the people, places it on the corporal, and genuflects in adoration. Then he sings or says:

Let us proclaim the mystery of faith:

All sing or say one of the following acclamations:

A Christ has died,
Christ is risen,
Christ will come again.

B Dying you destroyed our death,
rising you restored our life.
Lord Jesus, come in glory.

C When we eat this bread and drink this cup,
we proclaim your death, Lord Jesus,
until you come in glory.

D Lord, by your cross and resurrection
you have set us free.
You are the Savior of the world.

With hands extended, the priest says:

Father, we celebrate the memory of Christ, your Son.
We, your people and your ministers,
recall his passion,
his resurrection from the dead,
and his ascension into glory;
and from the many gifts you have given us
we offer to you, God of glory and majesty,
this holy and perfect sacrifice:
the bread of life
and the cup of eternal salvation.

Look with favor on these offerings
and accept them as once you accepted
the gifts of your servant Abel,
the sacrifice of Abraham, our father in faith,
and the bread and wine offered by your priest Melchisedech.

Bowing, with hands joined, he continues:

Almighty God,
we pray that your angel may take this sacrifice
to your altar in heaven.
Then, as we receive from this altar
the sacred body and blood of your Son,

He stands up straight and makes the sign of the cross, saying:

let us be filled with every grace and blessing.

He joins his hands.

[Through Christ our Lord. Amen.]

With hands extended, he says:

Remember, Lord, those who have died
and have gone before us marked with the sign of faith,
especially those for whom we now pray, N. and N.

The priest prays for them briefly with joined hands. Then, with hands extended, he continues:

May these, and all who sleep in Christ,
find in your presence
light, happiness, and peace.

He joins his hands.

[Through Christ our Lord. Amen.]

With hands extended, he continues:

For ourselves, too, we ask
some share in the fellowship of your apostles and martyrs,
with John the Baptist, Stephen, Matthias, Barnabas,

[Ignatius, Alexander, Marcellinus, Peter,
Felicity, Perpetua, Agatha, Lucy,
Agnes, Cecilia, Anastasia,]

and all the saints.

He strikes his breast with the right hand, saying:

Though we are sinners,
we trust in your mercy and love.

With hands extended, he continues:

Do not consider what we truly deserve,
but grant us your forgiveness.

He joins his hands.

Through Christ our Lord.

He continues.

Through him you give us all these gifts.
You fill them with life and goodness,
you bless them and make them holy.

He takes the chalice and the paten with the host and, lifting them up, sings or says:

Through him, with him, in him,
in the unity of the Holy Spirit,
all glory and honor is yours, almighty Father,
for ever and ever.

The people respond:

Amen.

Communion Rite, page 43.

The priest, with hands extended, says:

Lord, you are holy indeed,
the fountain of all holiness.

He joins his hands. Then, holding them outstretched over the offerings, he says:

Let your Spirit come upon these gifts to make them holy,
so that they may become for us

He joins his hands and, making the sign of the cross once over both bread and chalice, says:

the body ✠ and blood of our Lord, Jesus Christ.

He joins his hands. The words of the Lord in the following formulas should be spoken clearly and distinctly, as their meaning demands.

Before he was given up to death,
a death he freely accepted,

He takes the bread and, raising it a little above the altar, continues:

he took bread and gave you thanks.
He broke the bread,
gave it to his disciples, and said:

He bows slightly:

Take this, all of you, and eat it:
this is my body which will be given up for you.

He shows the consecrated host to the people, places it on the paten, and genuflects in adoration. Then he continues:

When supper was ended, he took the cup.

He takes the chalice and, raising it a little above the altar, continues:

Again he gave you thanks and praise,
gave the cup to his disciples, and said:

He bows slightly.

Take this, all of you, and drink from it:
this is the cup of my blood,
the blood of the new and everlasting covenant.
It will be shed for you and for all
so that sins may be forgiven.
Do this in memory of me.

He shows the chalice to the people, places it on the corporal, and genuflects in adoration. Then he sings or says:

Let us proclaim the mystery of faith:

All sing or say one of the following acclamations:

A Christ has died,
Christ is risen,
Christ will come again.

B Dying you destroyed our death,
rising you restored our life.
Lord Jesus, come in glory.

C When we eat this bread and drink this cup,
we proclaim your death, Lord Jesus,
until you come in glory.

D Lord, by your cross and resurrection
you have set us free.

You are the Savior of the world.

With hands extended, the priest says:

In memory of his death and resurrection,
we offer you, Father, this life-giving bread,
this saving cup.
We thank you for counting us worthy
to stand in your presence and serve you.
May all of us who share in the body and blood
of Christ
be brought together in unity by the Holy Spirit.

Lord, remember your Church throughout the world;
make us grow in love,
together with N. our pope,
N. our bishop,

(or N. our bishop and his assistant bishops,)

and all the clergy.

In Masses for the dead, the following may be added:

Remember N., whom you have called from this life.
In baptism he (or she) died with Christ:
may he (or she) also share his resurrection.

Remember our brothers and sisters
who have gone to their rest
in the hope of rising again;
bring them and all the departed
into the light of your presence.
Have mercy on us all;
make us worthy to share eternal life
with Mary, the virgin Mother of God,

with the apostles, and with all the saints
who have done your will throughout the ages.
May we praise you in union with them,
and give you glory

He joins his hands.

through your Son, Jesus Christ.

He takes the chalice and the paten with the host and, lifting them up, sings or says:

Through him, with him, in him,
in the unity of the Holy Spirit,
all glory and honor is yours, almighty Father,
for ever and ever.

The people respond:

Amen.

Communion Rite, page 43.

III Eucharistic Prayer

The priest, with hands extended, says:

Father, you are holy indeed,
and all creation rightly gives you praise.
All life, all holiness comes from you
through your Son, Jesus Christ our Lord,
by the working of the Holy Spirit.
From age to age you gather a people to yourself,
so that from east to west
a perfect offering may be made
to the glory of your name.

He joins his hands and, holding them outstretched over the offerings, says:

And so Father, we bring you these gifts.
We ask you to make them holy by the power of your Spirit,

He joins his hands and, making the sign of the cross once over both bread and chalice, says:

that they may become for us the body ✠ and blood
of your Son, our Lord Jesus Christ,
at whose command we celebrate this eucharist.

He joins his hands and speaks the words of the Lord clearly and distinctly, as their meaning demands.

On the night he was betrayed,

He takes the bread and, raising it a little above the altar, continues:

he took bread and gave you thanks and praise.
He broke the bread, gave it to his disciples, and said:

He bows slightly.

Take this, all of you, and eat it:
this is my body which will be given up for you.

He shows the consecrated host to the people, places it on the paten, and genuflects in adoration. Then he continues:

When supper was ended, he took the cup.

He takes the chalice and, raising it a little above the altar, continues:

Again he gave you thanks and praise,
gave the cup to his disciples, and said:

He bows slightly.

Take this, all of you, and drink from it:
this is the cup of my blood,
the blood of the new and everlasting covenant.
It will be shed for you and for all
so that sins may be forgiven.
Do this in memory of me.

He shows the chalice to the people, places it on the corporal, and genuflects in adoration. Then he sings or says:

Let us proclaim the mystery of faith:

All sing or say one of the following acclamations:

A Christ has died,
Christ is risen,
Christ will come again.

B Dying you destroyed our death,
rising you restored our life.

Lord Jesus, come in glory.

C When we eat this bread and drink this cup,
we proclaim your death, Lord Jesus,
until you come in glory.

D Lord, by your cross and resurrection
you have set us free.
You are the Savior of the world.

With hands extended, the priest says:

Father, calling to mind the death your Son endured for our salvation,
his glorious resurrection and ascension into heaven,
and ready to greet him when he comes again,
we offer you in thanksgiving this holy and living sacrifice.

Look with favor on your Church's offering,
and see the Victim whose death has reconciled us to yourself.
Grant that we, who are nourished by his body and blood,
may be filled with his Holy Spirit,
and become one body, one spirit in Christ.

May he make us an everlasting gift to you
and enable us to share in the inheritance of your saints,
with Mary, the virgin Mother of God,
with the apostles, the martyrs,

(Saint N. — the saint of the day or the patron saint)

and all your saints,
on whose constant intercession we rely for help.

Lord, may this sacrifice,
which has made our peace with you,
advance the peace and salvation of all the world.
Strengthen in faith and love your pilgrim Church on earth;
your servant, Pope N., our bishop N.,

(or N. our bishop and his assistant bishops,)

and all the bishops,
with the clergy and the entire people your Son has gained for you.
Father, hear the prayers of the family you have gathered here before you.
In mercy and love unite all your children wherever they may be.

Welcome into your kingdom our departed brothers and sisters,
and all who have left this world in your friendship.

He joins his hands.

We hope to enjoy forever the vision of your glory,
through Christ our Lord, from whom all good things come.

When this eucharistic prayer is used in Masses for the dead, the following may be said:

Remember N.
In baptism he (or she) died with Christ:
may he (or she) also share his resurrection,
when Christ will raise our mortal bodies
and make them like his own in glory.

Welcome into your kingdom our departed brothers
and sisters,
and all who have left this world in your friendship.
There we hope to share in your glory
when every tear shall be wiped away.
On that day, we shall see you, our God, as you are.

He joins his hands.

We shall become like you
and praise you for ever through Christ our Lord,
from whom all good things come.

He lifts the paten and the chalice, singing or saying:

Through him, with him, in him,
in the unity of the Holy Spirit,
all glory and honor is yours,
almighty Father, for ever and ever.

The people respond:

Amen.

Communion Rite, page 43.

IV Eucharistic Prayer

The priest, with hands extended, says:

Father, we acknowledge your greatness:
all your actions show your wisdom and love.
You formed man in your own likeness
and set him over the whole world
to serve you, his creator,
and to rule over all creatures.
Even when he disobeyed you and lost your friendship
you did not abandon him to the power of death,
but helped all men to seek and find you.
Again and again you offered a covenant to man,
and through the prophets taught him to hope for salvation.
Father, you so loved the world
that in the fullness of time you sent your only Son to be our Savior.
He was conceived through the power of the Holy Spirit,
and born of the Virgin Mary,
a man like us in all things but sin.
To the poor he proclaimed the good news of salvation,
to prisoners, freedom,
and to those in sorrow, joy.
In fulfillment of your will
he gave himself up to death;
but by rising from the dead,
he destroyed death and restored life.
And that we might live no longer for ourselves but for him,
he sent the Holy Spirit from you, Father,
as his first gift to those who believe,

to complete his work on earth
and bring us the fullness of grace.

He joins his hands and, holding them outstretched over the offerings, says:

Father, may this Holy Spirit sanctify these offerings.

He joins his hands and, making the sign of the cross once over both bread and chalice, says:

Let them become the body ✠ and blood of Jesus
Christ our Lord

He joins his hands.

as we celebrate the great mystery
which he left us as an everlasting covenant.

The words of the Lord in the following formulas should be spoken clearly and distinctly, as their meaning demands.

He always loved those who were his own in the
world.
When the time came for him to be glorified by you,
his heavenly Father,
he showed the depth of his love.

While they were at supper,

He takes the bread and, raising it a little above the altar, continues:

he took bread, said the blessing, broke the bread,
and gave it to his disciples, saying:

He bows slightly.

Take this, all of you, and eat it:
this is my body which will be given up for you.

He shows the consecrated host to the people, places it on the paten, and genuflects in adoration. Then he continues:

In the same way, he took the cup filled with wine.

He takes the chalice and, raising it a little above the altar, continues:

He gave you thanks and, giving the cup to his disciples, said:

He bows slightly.

Take this, all of you, and drink from it:
this is the cup of my blood,
the blood of the new and everlasting covenant.
It will be shed for you and for all
so that sins may be forgiven.
Do this in memory of me.

He shows the chalice to the people, places it on the corporal, and genuflects in adoration. Then he sings or says:

Let us proclaim the mystery of faith:

All sing or say one of the following acclamations:

A Christ has died,
Christ is risen,
Christ will come again.

B Dying you destroyed our death,
rising you restored our life.
Lord Jesus, come in glory.

C When we eat this bread and drink this cup,
we proclaim your death, Lord Jesus,
until you come in glory.

D Lord, by your cross and resurrection
you have set us free.
You are the Savior of the world.

With hands extended, the priest says:

Father, we now celebrate this memorial of our redemption.
We recall Christ's death, his descent among the dead,
his resurrection, and his ascension to your right hand;
and, looking forward to his coming in glory,
we offer you his body and blood,
the acceptable sacrifice
which brings salvation to the whole world.

Lord, look upon this sacrifice which you have given to your Church;
and by your Holy Spirit, gather all who share this one bread and one cup
into the one body of Christ, a living sacrifice of praise.

Lord, remember those for whom we offer this sacrifice,
especially N. our Pope,
N. our bishop,

(or N. our bishop and his assistant bishops,)

and bishops and clergy everywhere.
Remember those who take part in this offering,
those here present and all your people,
and all who seek you with a sincere heart.
Remember those who have died in the peace of Christ
and all the dead whose faith is known to you alone.
Father, in your mercy grant also to us, your children,
to enter into our heavenly inheritance
in the company of the Virgin Mary, the Mother of God,

and your apostles and saints.
Then, in your kingdom, freed from the corruption of sin and death,
we shall sing your glory with every creature through Christ our Lord,

He joins his hands.

through whom you give us everything that is good.

He takes the chalice and the paten with the host and, lifting them up, sings or says:

Through him, with him, in him,
in the unity of the Holy Spirit,
all glory and honor is yours, almighty Father,
for ever and ever.

The people respond:

Amen.

Communion Rite, page 43.

Communion Rite

The priest sets down the chalice and paten and, with hands joined, sings or says one of the following:

A Let us pray with confidence to the Father
in the words our Savior gave us.

B Jesus taught us to call God our Father,
and so we have the courage to say:

C Let us ask the Father to forgive our sins
and to bring us to forgive those who sin against us.

D Let us pray for the coming of the kingdom
as Jesus taught us.

The Lord's Prayer

The priest extends his hands and continues, with the people:

Our Father, who art in heaven,
hallowed be thy name;
thy kingdom come;
thy will be done on earth as it is in heaven.
Give us this day our daily bread;
and forgive us our trespasses
as we forgive those who trespass against us;
and lead us not into temptation,
but deliver us from evil.

With hands extended, the priest continues alone:

Deliver us, Lord, from every evil,
and grant us peace in our day.
In your mercy keep us free from sin
and protect us from all anxiety
as we wait in joyful hope
for the coming of our Savior, Jesus Christ.

He joins his hands.

Doxology

The people end the prayer with the acclamation:

For the kingdom, the power, and the glory are yours,
now and for ever.

Sign of Peace

Then the priest, with hands extended, says aloud:

Lord Jesus Christ, you said to your apostles:
I leave you peace, my peace I give you.
Look not on our sins, but on the faith of your Church,
and grant us the peace and unity of your kingdom,

He joins his hands.

where you live for ever and ever.

The people respond:

Amen.

The priest, extending and joining his hands, adds:

The peace of the Lord be with you always.

The people respond:

And also with you.

Then the deacon (or the priest) may add:

Let us offer each other a sign of peace.

All make an appropriate sign of peace, according to local custom. The priest gives the sign of peace to the deacon or minister.

The Breaking of the Bread

Then the following is sung or said by all:

Lamb of God, you take away the sins of the world:
have mercy on us.

Lamb of God, you take away the sins of the world:
have mercy on us.

Lamb of God, you take away the sins of the world:
grant us peace.

This may be repeated until the breaking of the bread is completed, but the last phrase is always grant us peace.

Meanwhile, the priest takes the host and breaks it over the paten. He places a small piece in the chalice, saying inaudibly:

May this mingling of the body and blood of our Lord Jesus Christ bring eternal life to us who receive it.

Private Preparation of the Priest

The people prepare themselves for receiving the body and blood of Christ by silent prayers of their own, for which no form is prescribed. Meanwhile, the priest joins his hands and says inaudibly:

Lord Jesus Christ, Son of the living God, by the will of the Father and the work of the Holy Spirit your death brought life to the world. By your holy body and blood free me from all my sins, and from every evil. Keep me faithful to your teaching, and never let me be parted from you.

Or:

Lord Jesus Christ, with faith in your love and mercy I eat

your body and drink your blood. Let it not bring me condemnation, but health in mind and body.

The Invitation to Communion

The priest genuflects. Taking the host, he raises it slightly over the paten and, facing the people, says aloud:

This is the Lamb of God
who takes away the sins of the world.
Happy are those who are called to his supper.

He adds, once only, with the people:

Lord, I am not worthy to receive you,
but only say the word, and I shall be healed.

He faces the altar and says inaudibly:

May the body of Christ bring me to everlasting life.

He reverently consumes the body of Christ, while the communion song is begun. Then he takes the chalice and says inaudibly:

May the blood of Christ bring me to everlasting life.

He reverently drinks the blood of Christ. After this he takes the paten or other vessel and goes to the communicants.

The National Conference of Catholic Bishops has issued the following guidelines for receiving communion.

For Catholics: As Catholics, we fully participate in the celebration of the eucharist when we receive Holy Communion. We are encouraged to receive communion devoutly and frequently. In order to be properly disposed to receive communion, participants should not be conscious of grave sin and normally should have fasted for one hour. A person who is conscious of grave sin is not to receive the body and blood of the Lord without prior sacramental confession except for a grave reason where there is no opportunity for confession. In this case, the person is to be mindful of the obligation to make an act of perfect contrition, including the intention of confessing as soon as possible (canon 916). A frequent reception of the Sacrament of Penance is encouraged for all.

For Our Fellow Christians: We welcome our fellow Christians to this celebration of the eucharist as our brothers and sisters. We pray that our common baptism and the action of the Holy Spirit in this eucharist will draw us closer to one another and begin to dispel the sad divisions that separate us. We pray that these will lessen and finally disappear, in keeping with Christ's prayer for us "that they may all be one" (Jn 17:21).

Because Catholics believe that the celebration of the eucharist is a sign of the reality of the oneness of faith, life, and worship, members of those churches with whom we are not yet fully united are ordinarily not admitted to holy communion. Eucharistic sharing in exceptional circumstances by other Christians requires permission according to the directives of the diocesan bishop and the provisions of canon law (canon 844 §4). Members of the Orthodox Churches, the Assyrian Church of the East, and the Polish National Catholic Church are urged to respect the discipline of their own Churches. According to Roman Catholic discipline, the Code of Canon Law does not object to the reception of Communion by Christians of these Churches (canon 844 §3).

For Those Not Receiving Communion: All who are not receiving holy communion are encouraged to express in their hearts a prayerful desire for unity with the Lord Jesus and with one another.

For Non-Christians: We also welcome to this celebration those who do not share our faith in Jesus. While we cannot admit them to holy communion, we ask them to offer their prayers for the peace and the unity of the human family.

The priest or other minister distributing the eucharistic bread takes a host for each communicant, raises it a little, and shows it, saying:

The body of Christ.

To which the communicant replies:

Amen.

and receives communion.

The host is received on the tongue or, in the United States, in the hand, at the option of the communicant. The priest or minister does not make the decision as to the manner of reception.

The sign of communion is more complete when the eucharist is given under both kinds, since the sign of the eucharistic meal appears more clearly. The intention of Christ that the new and eternal covenant be ratified in his blood is better expressed, as is the relation of the eucharistic banquet to the heavenly banquet.

If the chalice is offered, the priest or other minister raises it before each communicant, saying:

The blood of Christ.

To which the communicant replies:

Amen.

and drinks from it.

The deacon and other ministers may receive communion from the chalice.

After the communion or after Mass, the vessels are cleansed, if possible at the side table, by the priest, the deacon, or an acolyte, who says inaudibly:

Lord, may I receive these gifts in purity of heart.
May they bring me healing and strength, now and for ever.

Period of Silence or Song of Praise

The priest may return to his chair. A period of silence may be observed, or a psalm or song of praise may be sung.

Prayer after Communion

Standing at the chair or at the altar, the priest sings or says:

Let us pray.

All pray in silence, unless a period of silence has already been observed. Then the priest extends his hands and sings or says the prayer after communion, at the end of which the people respond:

Amen.

Concluding Rite

If there are any brief announcements, they are made at this time. Then, standing and facing the people, the priest extends his hands and sings or says:

The Lord be with you.

The people respond:

And also with you.

A Simple blessing

Priest: May almighty God bless you,
the Father, and the Son, ✠ and the Holy Spirit.

People: Amen.

On certain days or occasions a solemn blessing or prayer over the people may be used as the rubrics direct.

B Solemn blessings follow this form, a form proper to the season or the intention of the Mass, or any of several variants given in the Roman Missal, at the discretion of the priest.

Priest or deacon: Bow your heads and pray for God's blessing.

Priest: May almighty God bless you,
the Father, and the Son, ✠ and the Holy Spirit.

People: Amen.

C Prayers over the people follow this form, a form proper to the season or the intention of the Mass, or any of several variants given in the Roman Missal, at the discretion of the priest.

Priest or deacon: Bow your heads and pray for God's blessing.

After the prayer over the people, the priest always adds:

May almighty God bless you,
the Father, and the Son, ✠ and the Holy Spirit.

The people respond:

Amen.

DISMISSAL

The dismissal sends each member of the congregation to do good works, praising and blessing the Lord.

The deacon (or the priest), with hands joined, sings or says:

A Go in the peace of Christ.

B The Mass is ended; go in peace.

C Go in peace to love and serve the Lord.

The people respond:

Thanks be to God.

From the Mass of the Easter Vigil through the Saturday after Easter, and on Pentecost Sunday:

Priest or deacon: The Mass is ended; go in peace, alleluia, alleluia.

People: Thanks be to God, alleluia, alleluia.

If any liturgical service is to follow immediately, the rite of dismissal is omitted.

The priest kisses the altar, makes the customary reverence with the ministers, and leaves.

A Ω